ADI PUCKETT

Graciously Diverse: A Mighty
Little Guide to Seeing & Loving
Our Neighbors

Love, Grace & Unity

A Puckett

This book was professionally typeset on Reedsy.

Find out more at reedsy.com

This mighty little book is dedicated to every woman who has ever mothered me - from birth to practical; from neighborly to spiritual. You are all bright stars in the sky of my life, and your lights have always led me rightly.

Contents

Foreword

WELCOME!

I am so glad you have decided to take this next step in the journey of your life. While there has always been a need for a book like this, the times we live in beg for loving and gracious perspective on the things that cause us so much pain, anxiety and fear. My hope is to alleviate some of the fears you, the reader, may have so that you can move forward with knowledge and a bold intent to use it wisely.

This simple eBook is a basic, but clear view of who we are as people, the decisions that drive our interactions with other human beings, and what we can do to correct our perspectives and love our neighbors rightly.

Acknowledgement

It is a pleasure to be able to acknowledge the following people:

Sara DeYoung: Thank you for being such a great old/new friend and shrewd proof-reader.

Pastor Jason Schifo: Thank you for being frustrated enough to light fires under me. You are more than a Pastor. You are a true friend.

Amanda Chrappa: It was your idea in the first place. Who knows what we'll come up with the next time we get together to eat cookies?

Franklin Puckett, Jr: My husband is more patient than I give him credit for. Thank you, dear.

Tamara Llano: The teacher always needs a teacher, and you are so good at what you do! Thank you SO BIG!

CEFC and Village of Mahomet, IL: The support and encouragement has been overwhelming, and I'll be forever grateful.

1
Diversified Us

"If even lifeless instruments, such as the flute or the harp, do not give distinct notes, how will anyone know what is played?"

-1 Corinthians 14:7

By definition, diversity simply means having a range of differences, and that could cover the options we have for many areas of our lives. In this case, however, this range of differences will apply only to people - the people we live, work, and play with.

Regardless of what we might see on the outside that we might consider similar or different, the differences that truly matter are often found on the inside of a person's mind, heart, and spirit.

Whatever we do with other people, we all notice external differences, but many of us don't acknowledge or address those differences for fear that our questions or comments may be seen as rude or ignorant. And so we continue to function alongside these different individuals without really knowing them beyond what they allow us to see or hear.

If we're honest, for one reason or another, we might actually be more comfortable being afraid than we would be with facing the fear and making our lives a little easier and happier. But sometimes, making our lives a little easier takes getting a little uncomfortable along the way. If we have a few bits of basic information to start with, however, it removes a lot of the discomfort.

While our differences are important, collectively, we are a reflection of the society we live in. America, aptly described as a giant melting pot, boasts one of the greatest spectacles of color and culture a person might ever see on earth.

We have physical attributes like skin color, hair texture, nose shape, and many more on a never ending list of distinguishing physical characteristics.

Then, there are the differences that cannot be seen. These details surround the things that make us more human than what we look like. We all have our religious (or non-religious) affiliations, our political stances, or other lifestyle choices that cannot be known unless shared or promoted in some way. Even simple preferences of foods or hobbies are usually unknown details.

One thing we all should consider is that diversity does not only refer to certain races, cultures or skin colors. Any attribute or quality that can be used to describe a human being makes them diverse. For the purposes of the information provided in this book, I invite us all to think of everyone who is not us as diverse, unique, and valuable.

When I meet a person I've never seen before, I have learned to consider that this person would like for me to treat them as if there is more to them than what I am hearing or seeing. It is my job to look for those unseen qualities that will allow me to treat them as 'more'.

If time is taken to look for and understand these differences, fear loses its hold, and we start to enjoy those differences instead of being wary of them.

Breathe In:

Before we get too deep, though, I'd like to offer a little grace. We are not all made up of the same experiences, so it is not healthy to expect yourself, or anyone else, to automatically see someone else's light. Let's give ourselves a bit of a break when it comes to the things we may not know or understand right away. Change takes time.

Try This:

- Put aside what you thought you knew.
- Think of a time when you were externally judged.
- Remember that feeling.
- Ask yourself what it would have taken to alleviate those feelings.

Breathe Out:

If you take a good look at your surroundings, you may observe other people going about their normal daily routines. As you watch, you may only assume the things that may be on their minds. From here on out, let's go ahead and assume that you are wrong. Every other human being on the planet is as complicated...or as simple...as you.

Because we are so human, we are so driven by what we hear and see, we often neglect to look deeper. For the rest of this e-book, I'd like to challenge you to give every other person (who comes to mind as you read) the same grace that you just gave yourself. They deserve it as much as you do.

MINDFULNESS:

In this section, you get to reflect on what you think about diversity, how you have responded to it, and how you feel about that.

Answer the following questions honestly. No one has to see the answers but you and God. The best part is that, fair or foul, He already knows and loves you desperately anyway.

- What is your first thought when you hear the word, 'diversity'?

- How many relationships do you have with people not like you?

- Do you behave differently around the diverse people in your life?

- Can you be gracious with yourself concerning what you don't know?

- What are some deep things you wish people knew about you?

2

Diversified Views

My Brothers, show no partiality as you hold the faith of our Lord,
Jesus Christ.
James 2:1

The opportunities available to the citizens of the United States of American are quite diverse, and that's a good thing. Access to these opportunities, however, are very diverse, and that is a problem. The label of this nation is *The land of Opportunity* - not for select races, socioeconomic statuses, or personalities - but for anyone who would dare put it to the test. Every single one of us cares about what kind of future we have or what

kind of legacies we will leave for our children. The desire for a prosperous, free, and happy life rests largely on the belief that America is the place to have it.

It's true. America really *is* the place - if you fit the description of what our society gives for who deserves it.

Since the death of George Floyd, there has been so much to read and listen to regarding the plight of the black human being. Even in my own home, there has been discord. My white husband had a hard time understanding what all the fuss was about because it felt to him that black America was blaming him for all our woes. If I'm honest, that's really what it can sound like, depending on the source. This left him feeling like he shouldn't say or do anything since he never knows how his words or deeds will be received.

My explanation to him was this: Said fuss breaks down to the fact that Mr. Floyd's manner of death was one of many straws, collected over centuries, that finally broke the camel's back. I feel very sorry for this poor camel, because this isn't the first time its poor back has been broken.

Since this new spark, book clubs are popping up everywhere online to discuss the written works of such authors as Robin DiAngelo[1] (Author of *White Fragility: Why It's So Hard for White People to Talk About Racism*) or Eduardo Bonilla-Silva[2] (Author of *White Supremacy & Racism in the Post Civil Rights Era*) who are very thorough in their explanations of white guilt and privilege. In fact, there is so much information available about how awful (intentionally or unintentionally) and oblivious white people are that there's no wonder why many are so afraid to ask serious questions or say what's on their minds.

How can anyone gain clarity when all they're being told is that they are the problem? All of that guilt and shame only widens the racial divide as people desperately look for ways to apologize by saying and doing things that generally add up to mere pity and pandering. In many cases, nothing is said or done because people grow tired of being accused or thrown in with others. This will not teach the building of relationships with the people they're being accused of being so awful to. Seriously, while racial issues are very sensitive, we do seem to be overcooking the grits when it comes to learning how to face and reckon with one another.

Arguments over monuments, flags, politics, viruses, and anything else we can think of to disagree over are happening all over social media, and these same arguments are happening in our homes to spread out into our communities and infect the whole world. To say the least, it is frightening that we, as

13

human beings, seem more concerned with the symptoms than the disease.

Let's just call it what it is. The disease is racism, and the resulting wounds are grossly infected. It is a curable disease, however, as long as we can learn to be honest about what we are really dealing with.

What we are all experiencing here is not some strange anomaly. Racism is a crisis of humanity rooted in sin. We, as human beings are predisposed to survive, to protect our hearts, minds, and bodies by any means that we understand, even if those means are wrong.

The racial issues in this country should not be boiled down to the beliefs that white people are just racist or that black people are just angry. These issues exist because we, as a collective, are *all* entitled.

It boggles the mind for anyone to assert that black people can't be racists or that we have no privilege. I beg to differ.

When a young black female student can walk into the Multi- Cultural Center[3] of her college and demand all the white people in the room leave because she's feeling uncomfortable, I'm whipping out my racist flag because it was just that - plain old racist. Her argument was that they [white students] already have places on campus they could go to. By virtue of her freedoms so carelessly exercised in the video, she also has plenty of other places she could be and *way* more productive things she could be doing. Honestly, if it were my child, she'd be trying to work out how she would be paying for the rest of her college years while also formally and *publicly* apologizing for dishonoring herself, her family, her peers, and her nation in such a way.

When things like this can happen in public and be shared throughout the interwebs without it being called out as blatantly

14

racist and entitled, we get a really good example of black privilege to treat someone like that and the white guilt it takes to allow it.

Let's be honest. If the races had been reversed, every black person in the room would have told "Karen" to have several seats...and she would have taken them.

This is not okay!

Privilege is not some characteristic singular to a specific race. Privilege isn't even a bad thing until it is used to place one's self as dominant over another based on superficial qualities (race, gender, etc.). Literally anyone can practice it.

Literally, no one should...Ever.

Racism will always be a thing as long as there is more than one race. Asking what we can do to eradicate it may very well be the wrong question.

The better question is, perhaps, how do we learn to see people as just people – beautiful and incredible people who happen to have been designed on different areas of a dynamic pigment and melanin spectrum (heads-up: God did NOT make any red, yellow, black or white people – this is just what *we* call each other)? Are we capable of the mindset that tells us that the person next to you is just a man or lady who just happens to be a particular shade of brown or tan? Many of us assume that we already do – that we already treat everyone the same and don't see color.

Not seeing color is one of our largest mistakes, because it robs the other person of the respect due to their culture while also robbing us of opportunities to learn more about the world around us. One of the best things about the differences in our color is that we get to know the whole person which should *include* their colors and the cultures that come along with them. Deciding how we treat people *because* of their color is where

15

we have gone terribly wrong in this battle. No one should be cool, articulate, or smart for a [insert color] person. We should all be seen beneath our skins so that the differences in our skins are respected and not judged.

So, going forward, let's not be color blind. Let's be color-conscious. People like to be fully seen.

MINDFULNESS:

In this section, you get to write your thoughts about racism, your experiences with it, and your perspective on the divisiveness of it.

Answer the following questions honestly. Remember: No one has to see the answers but you and God. The best part is that, fair or foul, He already knows and loves you desperately anyway.

- What is your reaction to reports of racist attacks (on any color)?
- Have you ever participated in racist speech or behavior?
- What are your true feelings about the racial imbalance in our nation?
- What may need to change about your perspective on race?

3
Diversified Learning

"It is time for parents to teach young people early on that in diversity, there is beauty and there is strength." -Maya Angelou

The society we live in teaches us a lot about how to see and respond to others. Just off the cuff, During my childhood, I heard many things about certain groups of people that were simply irresponsible and unfair.

For example: White people are rich. Black people are dirty. Indians smell weird. Mexicans are lazy. Chinese people are smart. The list could go on and on!

The part that mesmerizes me is that I've met each and every one of these races, and every single one is true...for this ONE white lady I met, this ONE black girl I used to know, or for that ONE smart Chinese kid. I also grew up with plenty of poor white kids, was friends with an Indian family who all seemed to smell amazing, and was a neighbor to a Mexican gentleman who worked three jobs and still managed to keep his landscaping in pristine condition. Twelve years later, and I'm still trying to get my flowers to look as full and happy as those of Mr. Miguel.

A lot of gratitude comes with these memories because it shows that the opportunity to shift one's perspective is always available if we just have the courage to accept them.

How we miss it:

More important than the society we live in is the house we live in. My grandmother always said that charity (love) begins at home, meaning that much of what we learn is first taught to us at home.

In the midst of social unrest, I have had several conversations that consist of confessions of biased and prejudiced things we grew up learning from a parent, teacher, pastor (you read that right), or close friend...all trusted sources of love, care, and information. We had no idea that we were receiving information from some hard or bitter hearts. How could we? We were kids.

And as kids, we did as we learned. When I was in the 7th grade, my gym class was given free rein on the adjoining football field. We were allowed to do whatever we liked (socialize, play, or just take a stroll along the perimeter) as long as we stayed in motion for the entire class period. A classmate and I chose the leisurely stroll for our exercise and spent our time chatting about normal girlish things.

Neither of us was prepared for three of our classmates to come running up to us in a rage.

While screaming that I needed to learn how to stick with my own color, these three girls beat me pretty badly. The girl I had been walking with was silent while the rest of the class cheered and laughed. What I remember most about all of this is that not only did my white 'friend' not offer me any assistance, but neither did any of my black classmates.

That last bit of information never even occurred to me until I was an adult. The point, however, is that this event taught me a lot about myself and the people I share this planet with. The biggest lesson was that we were all victims.

Not a single one of us had an awareness of where this event would take us, the damage it might do, or the healing that could actually come from it later in life.

The only thing I was one hundred percent sure of was that while efforts can be appreciated, the request for me to stop loving and showing interest in people was irrevocably denied.

The very next lesson I received was from my grandmother who dressed my wounds and mended my torn clothing. She told me she had a question, but I would be required to think about it before answering.

Her question: "If you really think about what just happened, are people really worth it to you?"

My eventual answer: "Yes, ma'am."

Her simple response: "Well then, don't stop." And with that said, she walked away.

Looking back, I am the most grateful for that moment, because if she had been angry, I would've been too hurt and angry to learn the art of grace. I would not have been prepared for the next thing.

There would be no staying home from school the next day. My mom was livid, but my grandmother asked her to hold her peace

- to wait and see if I had the courage of my convictions. She knew that the price of grace is choosing humility over vengeance, even if vengeance is deserved. She also knew how hard that would be for 12-year old Me.

Fortunately for all concerned, it was one of the least eventful days of my middle school career. I can't recall talking about it with anyone after that. I remained myself - as unchanged and determined as I ever was.

Almost every decision I make about people is rooted in this sequence of events. They would be my first examples of grace and mercy triumphing over judgment.

66

The Price of Grace

is Choosing Humility

Over Vengeance

Two of the girls involved in this nasty piece of history are now my friends. Apologies have been made. Forgiveness has been extended and accepted. We understand that while this happened in our childhoods, our adulthoods require better of us. The old adage one can't teach an old dog new tricks really only applies to literal dogs. We adults learn what we want to learn.

Our biases, implicit or otherwise, can be changed - if we want them to. Nowadays, there are so many resources available to teach us about our biases and prejudices in ways that can definitely inspire growth in areas we never thought could change. We have to want to do it, though. We have to want to sign up for such classes as *Understanding Diversity & Inclusion* from Purdue University[4] (this one is free) or attend available workshops that offer practical application of the same subject like *Diverse Roots: Included Branches*[5], the companion workshop to this book.

A quick Google search for "racial justice training" or other such keywords can get you a laundry list of resources (some free, and some not) to help you learn how to engage in healthy conversations, approach delicate topics with diplomacy, see our world differently, and love our neighbors rightly.

On the note of loving our neighbors rightly as commanded in *Matthew 22: 37-39*[6], let's walk away from the notion of bashing this into the heads of those who don't believe as we do. Condemnation is not our job. Our job is to love even those who are not equipped with the same understanding. Instead of making 'love thy neighbor' a command from us, perhaps we can literally love our neighbors (believing or unbelieving) by walking alongside them as they make their way through learning and attempting to correct their own biases. The rejection of these precious hearts is already a very active part of our lines of division. This is not like God.

MINDFULNESS:

In this section, you get to think back as far as you can and write about your experiences with learning about the world around you. This is not an easy one, but it's worthy work.

Answer the following questions honestly. Remember: No one has to see the answers but you and God. The best part is that, fair or foul, He already knows and loves you desperately anyway.

- Who were your biggest influences in racial matters?

- What did they teach you about people of different races?

- How did you apply what you learned as you aged?

- Have your perceptions changed? If so, how have they changed?

- What resources are you taking advantage of to help you?

4

Diversified Relationships

"Friendship is born at that moment when someone says to another, "What? Me too! I thought I was the only one'."

-C.S. Lewis

Every one of us wants to be considered worthy of fair treatment. We all want to be respected and offered the same opportunities to thrive as anyone else, and we want to pursue these opportunities uninterrupted.

When we become so focused on a person's external presentation, we rob ourselves of our abilities to think critically about that person *as* a person. When we see a homeless person, we may only see a bum. When we see a man in a suit, we may only see success. Since September 11, 2001, a Middle-Eastern person is probably a terrorist. The angry white lady in the department store is guaranteed to be a soccer mom named Karen.

The young black man in the hoodie and saggy pants has got to be a thug with no father.

The only reason any of us would look at any of these individuals and have these be our first thoughts is because this is how each of them has been presented to us by the sources we have come to trust - parents, friends, leaders, news outlets, social media, etc. We learn the languages of our sources and regurgitate what we've learned when it's time to express how we feel about the things going on in the world, whether those things affect us personally or not.

AUTHENTICITY:

Something else our society has taught us is to be less of ourselves and more of what we think will be socially acceptable. In all of our efforts to not be considered 'basic', we sure have learned how to be more complicated than we have ever needed to be as people.

In our desire to not be rejected, we learn that it is, somehow,

better to be accepted in our false coverings than it is to be comfortable in the skin, hair, affinities, skill sets, and mannerisms we came into the world with. We learn to assimilate to avoid ridicule, abandonment, or any other abuse that comes with not fitting in.

Who made the rules of assimilation, though?

Whose idea was it that the only hairstyles acceptable in the workplace are silky, glossy locks for women and short cuts for men? Who dictated that the Southern American accent sounds ignorant next to that of an English accent? Where is it etched in stone that the college-educated person is guaranteed to be more intelligent than the vocationally trained person? Who was the first to say that to be white was good and clean, but to be black was to be bad and unclean?

A better question is this: when did we start blindly accepting these things as truths to live by? As sentient beings with full mental and physical autonomy, it hardly makes sense that we would find any of the above-mentioned details fair to all people in our melting pot. "Not like us" is not, and has never been, an acceptable reason to perceive or treat a person as *less* of a person. When our thoughts about a person dictate how we treat them, we automatically step out of simple, harmless bias and start taking a walk through the dark world of prejudice.

A prejudice is an unreasonable opinion formed with no real logic or experience, It is an opinion based on influenced emotion

26

rather than intelligent thought. It is, therefore, the epitome of perishing due to a lack of knowledge. This brings us back to sentience and autonomy. Do we only want to be seen as sentient and autonomous beings, or do we really want to *be* those things?

Our sentience and autonomy are comprised of those unseen characteristics we talked about in the first chapter.

Our power to think for ourselves creates a diversity that Malcolm Forbes, a former politician for the state of New York, calls "the art of thinking independently together".

This points out the greatest benefit to diversity which is relationship.

A special kind of comfort comes with knowing that my best friend of almost 40 years is hardly anything like me. Of all the things two people can have in common, we only share two passions: coffee and yarn. Otherwise, we are as different as night and day

She is white. I am black. She married young and is still with that man 20+ years later. I'm on my second marriage. She has two children. I have one. If Green Acres had a mascot, she would be it! Meanwhile, my husband can't even get me to go camping. Her in-laws are Rebels. Mine are definitely Patriots.

How did we get so close? It's simple. We learned about one another because we *wanted* to know one another. We knew what others wanted our relationship to look like, but our decision was (and still is) to allow the other person to be themselves while we stay ourselves.

66
Diversity is the Art
of Thinking
Independently
Together.

Same...Not Same:

Being honest and comfortable with yourself is often a good first step to learning how to be honest and comfortable with others. As we navigate the waters of a very difficult 2020, it can be very tempting to keep our eyes on the surface issues that immediately grab our attention in ways that make us feel compelled to respond with our gut reactions.

Our gut reactions come easily, but aren't always very bright.

Our emotions can lead us all over the place, and the fact that we all have them makes them even harder to navigate.

Checking those emotions at the door of a conversation, however, creates space in our minds for the logic that it takes to meet other people where they are and to see them *as* they are.

We can call this a lesson in finding common ground, but it's more accurate to call this a practice in empathy.

Empathy is such a special quality because it allows us to see exactly what's in front of us while also looking for a way to relate to it.

We are all so much the same in ways that we don't think much about. While our society might like for us to focus on our superficial differences, we often miss the ones that matter. The struggle, my dears, is real.

The struggles of race, economics, and society as a whole belong to all of us. None of us have cornered the market on it. It is, therefore, never necessary to dismiss the one person's struggle because you can't identify or sympathize with it. Instead, if we truly want to be united, taking the time to understand the effect the struggle has on the other person will take us a long way.

Struggle frightens us, hurts us, and often drives us a little insane (I'm being nice). The point is that the person next to you hurts just like you do when the world is unfair, worries when the bills are tight, cries over their children, and hopes for a good future.

It isn't necessary to always know what someone is going through as long as we can acknowledge that a struggle - whatever it is - exists and the person you're encountering is trying to survive it. And it's not easy.

Acknowledging that life is just as hard for someone else as it is for you will help you build bigger pictures of the people you interact with.

In my church, we have a decent amount of teenage girls who, for years, never really talked to one another, spent time together, or anything. A friend of mine and I thought this was unacceptable - to be united in faith without the actions of faith toward one another. After much observation and planning, we built a ministry that would put these girls together in marginally uncomfortable situations that would create a sense of awareness among them.

They work together to assist older women in the community. They play games that reveal deep details about themselves. They have hard conversations that make them vulnerable to one another. They have understandings that they would not have had if we had not created a safe environment to help them do so.

The eventual result of all that uncomfortable learning is now one pew full of curly-haired girls (two Latinas, two white, one biracial) who we now can't figure out how to silence during the sermon. More young ladies are scattered throughout the congregation, but that one pew just cracks us up! We are not angry at the beautiful monster we created, though. The Mary & Martha Project did its job well, because not only do these girls now have comrades and confidants, the services they offer to the older women of the church have also gained them a host of wise church mothers who can counsel and help them in times of need.

The struggles will never be easy, but now, they no longer feel they have to do it alone.

One of the primary reasons this project was started is because we realized something was out of sync in our church - our church *home - our house.*

Whether it is your residence, your church, your company, or your community, that place is *Your House.* Everyone in your house has their own gifts and skills to contribute to the running of that house. It is your responsibility to honor, respect, and protect the people in it. If you are in a position of authority in this house of yours, it is up to you to find out what everyone can contribute and combine them with your own efforts for a safe, welcoming, and beautifully diversified environment.

Remember: diversity is not only about color or any other outside human packaging. It takes everything that makes us human beings - on the inside - to live this life together.

MNDFULNESS:

In this section, you get to be honest about whether or not you judge others, how you feel about being judged, and what it has taken to move past those judgments.

Answer the following questions honestly. Remember: No one has to see the answers but you and God. The best part is that, fair or foul, He already knows and loves you desperately anyway.

- Have you ever judged based on appearance? Do you still?

- Have you ever changed to avoid being externally judged?

- What common struggles do you believe you share with others?

- Do you have relationships born of mutual struggle?

- Think of the people in "your house(s)". What can you learn from them?

5

Diversified Truth

"Have we not all one Father? Has not one God created us? Why then are we faithless to one another, profaning the covenant of our fathers? " Malachi 2:10

Loving all people is risky business. The desire to learn from and enjoy the company of those not like me has brought verbal and physical injury from many white people while also bringing alienation and abandonment by many black people...even some family.

None of this has kept me from seeking out opportunities to learn about the world around me, and it never will.

People are simply worth it to me...all of them. But allow me to make something very clear. My love of all people takes nothing away from the fact that I am indeed black and exceedingly proud of my melanin content and jubilant, boisterous culture. I need to point this out because, somehow, some members of the black race consider my graciousness to be synonymous with hating my own race. No, I don't get it either, but there you have it.

I know my history, and I take the time to stay informed so that I'm careful about what falls out of my mouth or off my fingertips. This being said, of course, I agree that black lives matter. I mean, I'm black. Why wouldn't I? I do, however, think the statement is incomplete.

As I've been listening, reading, and watching, I've observed many calls to change the narrative, and I've made that call myself.

#wordsmatter, and I am just as guilty as anyone when I put them out there for all to read or hear. Not everyone is a word nerd, but the structure of our spoken and written language requires that we use it carefully and clearly.

There is, however, a particular narrative that we're having a bit of trouble getting across. And I think I understand why. Many white people, depending on their surroundings, experiences, and upbringings just don't get it.

In a recent conversation, an acquaintance gave me all her reasons as to why so many, who cannot relate, continue to say that all lives matter. The reason that sticks out the most is: because, "We just don't get it!" was repeated several times within the conversation.

In my efforts to help her "get it", I informed her that the black race is one of the few races that has had to drag itself up from being considered and treated as less than animals. Even from the time of our emancipation, we have needed the help of small pockets of white people to beg other white people to accept us... to prove that we're okay - that we're just as capable, intelligent, creative, etc. as white people.

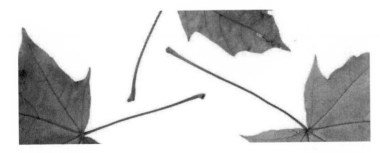

We should not need the permission of anyone to practice our inalienable rights uninterrupted...to enjoy life, liberty, and the pursuit of happiness without being asked if we're sure we belong in this neighborhood, that store, on this street, or in that professional position.

It should not come as a shock to a white teacher that a black student aces a test. It should not surprise a white person when a black person opens their mouth and intelligence flows from it.

My daughter should never have been told by her peers that she's just "white enough to fit in". I should never have been told "if I had met a black girl like you, I'da probably jumped the fence for you *wink*". Seriously, this was a white guy who had "never seen anything like" me before. What?!

We are not museum exhibits. We are not aliens from another planet. We are not modern marvels. We are not monkeys that seem to have, somehow, become receptive to training. We are simply human beings. From the hood to the suburbs, WE. ARE. PEOPLE!

All lives definitely do matter, but every life isn't crying out for an end to well over four centuries worth of abuse, disrespect, dismissal, patronization, and pandering. Every life hasn't been oppressed to the point of anger, grief, and exhaustion. Black lives have.

And we're tired of living in that space. It is not our home.

A SIMPLE TAKE-AWAY:

We are asking for people to see that we really are JUST intelligent, JUST capable, JUST beautiful, JUST creative, JUST lovable, JUST human.

There isn't a single one of us who is a rare find just because we might be into the same things someone else might be into. No one's level of comfort should dictate who or what others think we ought to be.

We're not trying to be accepted in a way that leads to sympathetic pandering.

We're asking for the empathy required for us to be accepted the way anyone else would like to be accepted as someone's parent, child, or friend - to not just be accepted or tolerated, but to be factually acknowledged to be a valuable part of this nation. So, to help change the narrative and use a tiny word that matters, I'm not going to tell you that #**blacklivesmatter**. I'm boosting a hashtag that has been largely ignored because it's simply not popular and doesn't pander to our overflowing emo- tions. I'm simply going to tell you that #**BlackLivesMatterToo.**

MINDFULNESS:

In this section, you get to reflect on your perception on the plight of the black race in our nation. Don't forget to give yourself grace for the things you don't understand. It's okay.

Answer the following questions honestly. Remember: No one has to see the answers but you and God. The best part is that, fair or foul, He already knows and loves you desperately anyway.

- What do you think it's like to be a person of color (POC) in the US?

- How much responsibility do you believe we bear in our struggles?

- Have you ever struggled to accept a POC into your life?

- Once accepted, what was your decision based on?

6

Diversified Action

*"Diversity may be the hardest thing for a society to live with, and
perhaps the most dangerous thing for a society to be without."*
-William Sloane Coffin, Jr.

Not very long after this current state of national unrest, I offered my services to speak at a Black Lives Matter rally that was happening in our fairly small village. It was very peaceful, well organized, and rather powerful. I can admit to feeling a little awkward, but that's normal when 98 percent of the people you are around are of a different race and you're feeling like your token presence finally has a purpose. What an awful time to feel one has purpose – to try to be the voice of hope in the faces of despair, outrage, and expectation.

The speech went awkwardly as well. While it was well prepared, I was not smart enough to use my smartphone to follow my bullet points like other speakers did. The wind was blowing, and the paper I unfolded from my pocket kept flapping and driving me up a wall. I kept losing my place, and the more I lost my place, the more nervous I became. I did not, however, miss providing my central point.

When I take stock of the words and actions of all of us on different areas of this issue, it occurred to me that something very needful was missing, but I couldn't quite put my finger on it.

In preparation, I ran across a section of scripture in the book of James that caught my attention. I jotted it down but didn't know how it directly related until a conversation occurred between me and my husband.

My poor husband did not want to go to the rally. He was feeling attacked in some way about the entire thing because there was a place in him that felt he was being blamed for the racism of others just because he is white. He felt lumped in. While it was a little hurtful that he didn't even want to go if only to support me, hearing how he felt crushed me even more.

It was like getting sloshed with ice water!

James 2:13 finally made sense and it brought tears to my whole self!

Someone needed to say they were sorry. Someone needed to forgive. So, this is the speech I really intended to give:

I do not know how any of you were raised. I do not know what your life experiences have been. I do not know what you harbor in your hearts. I do know the experiences that I have had in this village since moving here in 2013, and too many of them have been unpleasant. As a collective, I forgive you.

I am aware that none of you know how I was raised. None of you know my life experiences. You have no idea what I harbor in my heart. But what I would like for you to know is that I am sorry that we live in a society that tailors us to live opposed to one another – that we (black people) have been so hurt and angry that you are now afraid to ask the questions you so desperately want to ask because you have no idea what is going to be taken as offensive. Many of us have made you just as unwelcome in our hearts as we feel we have been in some of yours. Can you please forgive us?

Can we start a new chapter here in this small village that has begun to diversify in so many ways? Can I invite you all to acknowledge that we didn't do this to ourselves – that a line has been forced between us that is not very wide and only allows our fingertips to touch so that we couldn't grab ahold of one another even if we wanted to?

*I looked for something powerful and meaningful to say at this rally, and the only thing I could come up with was this little verse from the words of my Father in Heaven: "**For judgment is without mercy to the one who has shown no mercy. Mercy triumphs over judgment** (James 2:13)."*

My dears, we cannot afford to live among one another without mercy. We can't rally together in truth without grace. We cannot forgive, learn, or grow without grace. If you are new to grace, it simply means to be granted unmerited, or unearned, favor (kindness,

41

compassion, love, empathy). Basically, *grace requires no payment upfront or otherwise. I can't listen to you, and you can't stand with me without this beautiful, powerful, and largely overlooked gift.*

So, I ask again: Will you start a new kind of revolution with me? Will you set your feet and push forward – toward this line of division. Can you throw a blanket of grace over what society has taught us and push until that line collapses under the weight of a people who refuse to be defeated by themselves – a people who walk, talk, live, love, laugh, and grow together against all odds?

Who has the courage of the convictions that led you here tonight?

" *Mercy Triumphs Over Judgment*

A Gracious Rebuttal:

After this speech, I managed to get over how badly I flubbed it and move on to the next thing. In the process, however, a question was raised.

A fellow coach wanted to know "What about grace *from* a racist to a person attacked by racism?

It stumped me for a second, and I had to call back with an answer after some thought. The answer was simple: "What about it?"

Everything about what we want from this world starts at our doorstep - not that of anyone else. If we are concerned with whether or not we will be getting respect, grace, or dignity, we will never have these things to give.

Grace is not the kind of resource that can be replenished from one human being to another.

This is because we do not naturally have grace. Such a gift can only be tapped into at its natural source, and that would be God. After all, Jesus is the only one who loves us, literally, to death.

By His Spirit, grace is abundant, but we have to use it to keep it going. Not everyone is going to understand this, but for those of us who do, we cannot fail to keep that glass full.

If we wait around to see who will be showing us grace today, we will miss opportunities to empathize, to encourage, and to inspire because we will be too busy worried about our own validation or vindication.

No one owes anyone grace. It is up to us whether or not we want to offer it.

I have to ask, though: What does it feel like when God chooses grace over what you deserve? I know...it feels GREAT!!

MINDFULNESS:

It takes vulnerability to invite others to be vulnerable. As embarrassed as I was, I thought my embarrassment worth sharing. In this section, you get to share yours as well.

Answer the following questions honestly. Remember: No one has to see the answers but you and God. The best part is that, fair or foul, He already knows and loves you desperately anyway.

- Have you ever spoken out against racism? If so, when and how?

- Have you ever felt that you didn't have the right to speak up?

- Does the current environment make you feel obligated to act?

- What tools do you have that could affect positive racial change?

7

Diversified Clarity

"Don't worry about other people's opinions of you. God never told you to impress people; only to love them. -Dave Willis

Within my small Midwestern village, there is a bit of confusion surrounding something we Christians seem to take for granted. The new school season is about to kick off, and a lot of things are going to be different this year. Not only do we have issues surrounding Covid-19, but now adjustments are being asked to be made in the teaching of history and anti-racism. School board meetings have lasted for hours at a time in attempts to get everyone on the same page about how all of these things will be accomplished, and somewhere in the fog of confusion, there has been a fairly consistent snag.

On more than one occasion loving our neighbors as ourselves has been offered as the bulk portion of the solution to racial injustices, bullying, and other forms of inhumanity. In every instance of this suggestion, there has been pushback that says that doing so is simply not enough to affect positive changes to systemic racism and inequality within our community.

To be honest, I also believe that loving our neighbors rightly is a gigantic step toward bridging the racial divide. However, I have to admit that it has taken me quite a bit of time to understand why the pushback against such a simple and kind principle is so present. After having several conversations with other citizens in the community, it has occurred to me that saying that we love our neighbors is a whole lot different from actually doing it. What we've been missing is the practical application of what it truly means to love our neighbors as ourselves.

As Christians, we bear a responsibility to everyone around us to live the life we profess to believe. Anything other than practicing what we preach is mere lip service and makes us disingenuous. The pushback, in my observation, is mostly from those who do not believe as we believe but are asking us to walk our talk. In their own ways, they are saying that if we truly believe this works, we should be able to prove it. So, for the sake of everyone involved (that would be all of us), I'd like to provide a breakdown of what 'loving your neighbor' looks like, where we got it from, and how we can all put it to good use.

Of course, we Christians get our instruction from the Holy Bible. There are many translations of it, and we each use the one that we best understand. Personally, I use several translations as I study. For this piece, I will be using the ESV (English Standard Version).

In our Bibles, the request to love our neighbors is not an empty one. In fact, it's actually not even a request. It is a commandment.

Mathew 22:36-40 describes a conversation between Jesus and a lawyer.

> *"Teacher, which is the great commandment in the Law?"*
>
> *"And he" [Jesus] "said to him, 'You shall love the Lord your God with all your heart and with all your soul and with all your mind. This is the great and first commandment. And the second is like it: You shall love your neighbor as yourself.'"*
>
> Jesus gives the importance of His statement in Mark 12:31
>
> *"There is no other commandment greater than these."*

Here's why. Love, as explained in 1 Peter 4:8[7], covers a multitude of sins. This means that, when applied correctly, love has the power to diminish all wrongs committed by anyone. This isn't saying that people can just run around doing whatever they please without consequences, but it is saying that we can choose how we treat people based on how much wrong we are willing

47

to love them through. What everyone needs to understand, though, is that this love business is SO hard! Yes, I said it. Loving everybody is hard work. I cannot allow it to be thought that we Christians somehow have this magic switch that flips when we accept Jesus, and we suddenly become these perfect, lofty beings who automatically know what love really is and always get it right. Trust me, we don't.

Life as a Christian requires us to do a lot of things that go against our human nature. We are tasked with loving our neighbor, practicing self-control, being gracious – in EVERY situation! I would be lying if I said I don't struggle with it. Sometimes, I could force myself into days of repentance in exchange for one opportunity to put someone in their place. It's never worth it, though. As hard and messy as love can be, people are worth it. We are all human and desire to be treated fairly. We don't, however, always have a clear view of how to go about treating everyone fairly.

Thank goodness for a comprehensive list of what love looks like.

Many of us have read or heard of 1 Corinthians 13:1-8, but I want to paraphrase it for the purpose of perspective.

No matter what we do, none of it will matter if we do not have love. Whether it's speaking up, educating ourselves, practicing our faiths, giving to the poor, or sacrificing ourselves, if love is not our basic motivation, we are wasting our time. We might make someone feel good for a moment, but the gain is woefully temporary. Love is faithfully enduring.

Love is *patient*: Being silent while someone else is talking, giving people time to think and process information, thinking before you act or speak, not being angry when things don't happen in the time frame you'd like, letting life be a process, etc.

Love is *kind*: Holding doors for the people behind you, picking things up that someone dropped, cleaning the table where you eat, complimenting someone on their shoes or achievement, offering an objective ear, being there when you'd rather be elsewhere, etc.

Love *does not boast*: Keeping your good deeds to yourself unless asked about them, being a good winner and a gracious loser, not filming and posting that time you give a homeless person a sandwich, etc.

Love *does not envy*: Not being upset when someone has something you don't have, congratulating others on their accomplishments, being a gracious loser (again), learn about new things you don't understand, etc.

Love *is not arrogant*: Being humble in your victories, putting your pride aside even when you're right, listening to understand, remembering to be grateful, etc.

Love *is not rude*: Being gracious in your answers to questions that might concern you, not saying anything if you don't have anything nice to say, controlling your facial expressions and body language, putting a lid on your gut reactions, etc.

Love *does not insist on its own way*: Not having that fit when you don't get what you want, adapting to the needs of the situation, being willing to compromise, considering the fact that your way is not the only way, etc.

Love *is not irritable*: Finding your calm before entering a stressful situation, choosing to walk away rather than argue, actively avoiding personal triggers, considering the fact that life is hard for everyone, etc.

Love *is not resentful*: Remembering to be grateful (again), learning how to forgive, allowing yourself to be forgiven, letting go of past wrongs, taking every situation on a case-by-case basis,

49

etc.

Love *does not rejoice in wrongdoing, but rejoices with the truth:* Acknowledging a truthful thing from someone you don't like, interrupting bullies, graciously calling out wrongful speech or behavior, standing up for the unpopular, etc.

Love *bears all things*: Not allowing everything to become a fight, walking away even when offended, understanding that every action has a root reason, etc.

Love *believes all things:* Accepting the struggles of others as belonging to them, validating the existence of another's feelings, separating the thoughts of others from your own when in conversation, etc.

Love *hopes all things*: Desiring good for everyone, looking for the best in everyone, expecting the best when preparing for the worst, actively practicing the change you want to see, etc.

Love *endures all things:* Working your way through hard encounters, knowing when to leave the past behind, choosing joy over anger, or vengeance.

Love *never fails:* The practice of the above definitions of love creates the atmosphere necessary for healthy relationships to prosper. While it is not necessary to have a ton of close friendships, it *is* necessary to keep our relations with one another civil and gracious.

* * *

Working backward through my Bible, I'd like to point out why God finds it so important for us to love our neighbors. Not everyone has an understanding of the depth of God's love for us. I believe, however, that his primary motivation for our existence is so that He can love us and be loved by us in return. As the creator, He could very well demand this love, but He would rather it be our choice. Choosing to love Him makes our love authentic and solidifies the relationship between us. And so, it should be with our relationships with one another.

For every relationship, there should be ground rules and boundaries. The commandment to love one another stems from the first-ever 'ground rules' given which are the 10 Commandments as listed in Exodus 20 and Deuteronomy 6. These commandments are guidelines by which we can all build enduring relationships and set healthy boundaries within them. To explain:

The first 4 Commandments give us guidelines and boundaries for our relationship with God.

1. ***You shall have no other gods before Me***. (God made us, loves us, cares for us, protects us, and has given us dominion over every other living species on the planet. There is nothing else worthy of being placed above the God of all creation.)

2. ***You shall not worship any carved images*** of ANYTHING, not even Me (God's power cannot be harnessed or controlled through any object, so there is no need to bother with statues of Him.)

3. ***You shall not take the Lord's name in vain.*** (Unless we are praying to or speaking about God, we should not use His name loosely, especially as part of a curse or swear. If it isn't holy, keep Him out of it.)

4. ***Remember the Sabbath and keep it holy.*** (We all love our mental health days, and we could very well consider this commandment as such. Even God, the creator of the universe, took time to rest and reflect over all He had done. In like fashion, He wants us to take care of ourselves, and a big part of that is taking at least one day per week to rest and reflect on all that God has done for us.)

51

The remaining 6 Commandments are guidelines and boundaries for our relationships with one another.

1. **Honor your father and your mother that your days may be long on the Earth.** (While many of our child-to-parent relationships are strained, honor is still required from us as children. This guideline is not easy to follow at times, but knowing its purpose helps.)

2. **You shall not murder.** (This is all about respect for the value of human life. God knows the difference between self-defense and homicide, and He wants us to understand it as well.)

3. **You shall not commit adultery.** (This guideline warns us against having physical and/or emotional relations with a person who is...)

a. Not your spouse

b. Someone else's spouse

4. **You shall not steal** (If it is not given, purchased, earned or inherited, leave it there.)

5. **You shall not bear false witness against your neighbor** (God is not a liar, and bearing His image, we should be delighted in the truth. One of the best ways to avoid lying — speculating, judging, bashing, gossiping, etc. - on your neighbor is to mind your own business. It is way more profitable for everyone to have conversations with one another than to assume we know things that we really don't.)

6. **You shall not covet your neighbor's house** (To covet is to desire and to desire is to be tempted. To be tempted is to consider action. From there, it is a whole train wreck. Sweep around your own front door, and let others sweep around theirs. If you like something that someone else has, go buy your own, but there is no benefit to being jealous or sour over someone having something that you don't.)

52

All of this is being shared to say that the position of the Christ- minded individual is not to only pray or to just passively observe with our hands folded in our laps. We are called to act, but our actions have guidelines attached. We see no need to be angry, force agendas, or inspire guilt. They weigh too much and are incredibly exhausting.

What we *can* do is include ourselves in the efforts being made within our communities. It is notable that many non-believing members of our community are attempting to do things that we believers have also been called to do. They are fighting against bullying and racism, advocating for special needs individuals, donating to charities, fighting for equity, and pushing for policy changes to benefit everyone. While we might not like some of the ways these topics are approached, that doesn't mean we get to dismiss them or avoid taking action ourselves. In fact, we too are asked to:

"Learn to do good; seek justice, correct oppression; bring justice to the fatherless, please the widow's cause." Isaiah 1:17

By this instruction, we should be helping our neighbors in this fight. We have powerful tools onboard that can add proper fuel to their efforts and help get things going in the right direction. We were never meant to oppose non-believers, but to instead, attract them to the love of Jesus by our own examples of that love.

There are way too many of us Christians butting heads with non- believers in this land. If we are arguing with one another, we are off course. If, however, we are using what we understand to walk alongside our neighbors without expectation of their seeing everything from our perspective, our relationships will become more solid, more enduring, and more productive.

To my non-believing friends and acquaintances, I am very sorry for the times I have been a bad example of my own beliefs. Please, forgive me and allow me to do my part in helping us all be the change we want to see. I have not always been gracious when you didn't understand, and I regret that. Instead of pushing my own narrative, I should have been more patient and more kind. You deserve better.

My intent is to do better – to show what loving my neighbor truly looks like in thought, in speech, and in action. I don't want to do it just because God commands me to do it. I want to do it because He loves me and I know He also loves you, too. Call me an old softy, but that's good enough for me.

8

Diversified Conclusion

"And people will come from east and west, and from north and south, and recline at table in the kingdom of God." -Luke 13:29

There are very few things that are easy about basic peopling. The same can be said about loving each and every person on the planet the way we'd like to be loved. In the end, however, the rewards will go to those who put in the work.

The work looks like this:

- Listening to understand
- Checking our beliefs against the truth of God's word.
- Putting your feelings aside for the sake of someone else's when it counts.
- Empathizing instead of sympathizing
- Separating people from actions

The rewards look like this:

- Mindfulness for us and the people we share this world with unity
- Community
- Authentic relationships
- Enduring peace of mind and a joyful spirit

REFLECTION:

In this season, it's hard to miss the multiple disagreements happening on social media, over the phone, and even in person. Some of us even seem to live for the adrenaline that comes with a good battle of wills. What if we all have it just a bit wrong? What if we are plying our tools to one another as weapons instead of using them to accomplish the things we are designed to do?

What if we acknowledge that we are each equipped to fill certain roles in this life? Our personalities often start out rather rough, and that's okay. But as we age, experience, and observe, the traits that define our personalities are meant to be refined.

We have a responsibility to one another, and that responsibility is respect - respect for perspective, experiences we are unaware of, qualifications that have nothing to do with text books, cultural aspects, etc.

We owe it to one another to acknowledge that we each have our own custom set of tools for living, working, playing, and fighting - together.

Doing "Your Part" is Simple:

- Put down the guilt and anger. You don't need them anymore. Besides, they are too heavy.
- Pick up some new perspective and practice looking at the world with it. Be as gracious as you want to receive grace...whether you receive it or not. Be honest with yourself first.
- Have the hard conversations
- Use your tools to build unity and maintain respect for the tools of others.

FULL - SERVICE GUT CHECK

I am a firm believer in checking my conscious on a regular basis. Doing so keeps me out of my feelings and helps me to stay aware of others around me. One way I manage this "gut check is to make a list of things I find myself convicted about. As I pray about each one, I place a mark next to it and continue on to the next. I repeat this process as often as is necessary, and I have to let you know that it's pretty regular. My loving suggestion is that we all find ways to make sure we are remaining self-aware so that we can truly see other people with depth and clarity.

While driving down the road, I saw this adorable sign stretched across the front of a business building that said, "We will make it through this!"

Of course, the sign was referring to Covid-19, but I believe it definitely applies to the topic of racial unrest as well. As long as we are willing to keep fighting the good fight, the people we share life with will not be forgotten, overlooked, or treated like the cause of the month.

The good fight will not always feel good. The price will often be heavy - a lost friend or loved one who is still too afraid to be vulnerable enough to learn new (and old) things, ridicule by peers, or accusations of weakness just because your choice is to fight with your heart and your mind instead of with anger or violence. Just know that I think you are mighty and strong.

My dears, you are learning to do the hardest thing a person can do, and that is to truly love your neighbor as yourself.

Notes

DIVERSIFIED VIEWS

1 https://play.google.com/store/books/details?pcampaignid=books_read_action&id=ZfQ3DwAAQBAJ

2 https://books.google.com/books?hl=en&lr=&id=rVcdyCYwnosC&oi=fnd&pg=PR7&dq=Eduardo+Bonilla-Silva&ots=R-kdRw7Yia&sig=HubEYIZb9BWnoT4JuLjTbDoQ#v=onepage&q=Eduardo%20Bonilla-Silva&f=false

3 View video here: https://youtu.be/fgvKCz5psbg

DIVERSIFIED LEARNING

4 Sign up here: https://www.futurelearn.com/courses/diversity-inclusion-awareness

5 https://root2branches.com/product/diversity-inclusion-training/

6 Matthew 22:37-39

> "Jesus said to him, 'You shall love the Lord your God with all your heart, with all your soul, and with all your mind.' This is *the* first and great commandment. And the *second* is like it: 'You shall love your neighbor as yourself.'"

DIVERSIFIED CLARITY

7 "Above all, keep loving one another earnestly, since love covers a multitude of sins." 1 Peter 4:8 (ESV)

About the Author

As the owner of Root To Branches Ministries, Adi helps people build authentic relationships with themselves, their families, and their communities.

Adi is a nationally certified life coach and serves as a missionary and community activist in Champaign County, IL.

Her most important titles, however, are wife to Franklin (of 7 years), mom to their blended children, co-spoiler of the family's Yorkie-poo, and just a woman saved by grace.

Adi mostly functions with coffee in hand, music playing, and a scattered mess of notebooks around her laptop...and the rest of the house.

You can connect with me on:

🌐 https://root2branches.com
🐦 https://twitter.com/root2branches
📘 https://facebook.com/root2branches
🔗 https://www.linkedin.com/in/adi-puckett-846a9538

Subscribe to my newsletter:

✉ https://root2branches.com

More From Adi Puckett: *UnSelf Confidence*